The Perfect Man

by
Heather
Down

0 43422 69575 1

Written by Heather Down
Cover illustration by Design Dynamics, Glen Ellyn, IL
Typography by Dmitry Feygin

Published by Great Quotations Publishing Co.,
Glendale Heights, IL

ISBN 1-56245-301-7

Library of Congress Catalog Number: 97-071658

Printed in Hong Kong

Introduction

Through the centuries humans have gone to great lengths in search of myths. Entire lifetimes have been squandered looking for the Fountain of Youth, Big Foot, Alien life forms and the Lochness Monster. I fear that I, too, have been entrapped in a search which has also been in vain. During my adult years I have wasted precious time, energy and money looking for the Perfect Man. After years of in-depth research I have come to the conclusion that this creature is, in fact, also mythical. Along with Zeus and Hercules, the Perfect Man only exists in one's mind, thus making him a god indeed.

Thank You to Ken and Gwen for their priceless thoughts.

Dedication:

This book is for all the men who know they are, think they are or wish they were perfect!

The Perfect Man....

– puts the toilet seat in down position after use so other members of his household don't have a near-drowning experience in the middle of the night.

– does not have to have complete and sole custody of the T.V. remote control.

7

– Brushes regularly
and knows
what floss is.

– does not
consider a
belch a
mating call.

– knows that flowers are not just for cross-pollination.

– does the 3 D's - dishes, diapers and delivery room.

11

– has a job.

– doesn't yell when you've finished off all the cookies.

13

– doesn't think that "You need your tires rotated" is a romantic statement.

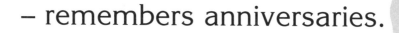 – remembers anniversaries.

– does not feel that he was divinely appointed to correct and punish poor drivers while on the freeway.

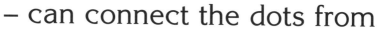 – can connect the dots from hamper to washer to dryer to ironing board to hanger.

17

– doesn't join a baseball team as an excuse to scratch himself in public.

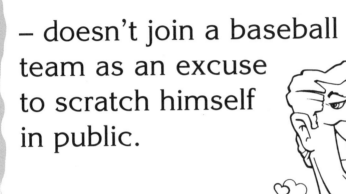

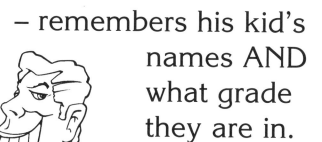

– remembers his kid's names AND what grade they are in.

– doesn't think grunting constitutes quality communication.

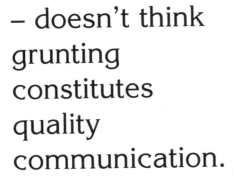

– doesn't think a
night out means a
Taco Bell
drive through.

21

– calls when he will be late.

– hates golf. Or if he does like it, does not insist that you play with him.

– likes to hug you even when he doesn't want sex.

– never uses the word "boink" to indicate making love.

– thinks that dogs, babies and hamsters are cute.

– packs his
own lunches.

– doesn't insist that
you attend every
one of his
ball games.

– thinks your nieces
are cute.

– doesn't laugh
when he sees
you naked.

– never refers to you as "old fart".

– doesn't think that cracking your toes is fun.

– does not confuse
the words
"love handles"
with "lovely".

– is always on time.

– does not use rude hand gestures while driving.

– knows that A&E is
a television channel.

– likes to hold hands.

– remembers his kid's birthdays.

– does not hog
the covers.

39

– remembers to put the garbage out and feed the dog.

– puts his family's bladders ahead of shortening the trip by 26 seconds.

– can say the words "I'm sorry".

– is willing to stop and ask
for directions.

43

– does not put the almost-empty juice container back into the fridge.

– does not read a map and drive at the same time.

– is willing to read the direction manual when setting up the VCR, computer or child's toy.

– watches more than just sports on T.V.

– does not think that chips and beer are essential food groups.

– knows when NOT to answer
your questions.

– does not drink directly out of the milk container.

– buys lingerie but doesn't wear it himself.

– not only takes phone messages, but gives them to you.

– unballs his socks before he puts them in the laundry hamper.

– realizes that the ideal romantic
getaway does not include
live bait.

– laughs at your jokes.

– is gentle.

– owns a suit….that still fits.

– keeps his dresser drawers in the "in" position.

– fills up the gas tank before exchanging cars.

– never uses the initials PMS
while engaged in an argument.

– knows how to wrap a present.

– is dexterous with dental floss, deodorant and dill.

– picks up milk, kids or dog food on the way home.

– goes to school concerts, little league games and teacher interviews.

– cuts his toe nails regularly and doesn't leave the clippings on the bathroom counter.

– knows the crucial difference between nylons and panty hose.

– doesn't think that reading the newspaper is an effective form of active listening.

– Knows how to turn on the vacuum cleaner, garbage disposal and you.

– uses foot powder.

– remembers Valentine's Day.

– doesn't steal extra mints
at restaurants.

– changes socks and underwear daily.

– limits his night out with the boys to once a week.

– barbecues.

– does not write telephone numbers, messages or important dates on scrap pieces of paper.

– is organized.

– can always find his shoes.

– is there for the birth as well as the conception.

– knows that can openers are not romantic presents.

– has an IQ higher than his age.

80

– does not have a bar stool permanently attached to his butt.

– gives a back massage that
provides relaxation
not paralyzation.

– believes in something other than organized sport or crime.

– does not name his body parts.

– definitely never names <u>your</u> body parts.

– phones before bringing
company home.

– is capable of transporting dishes from T.V. to sink.

– not only plants a garden, but pulls the weeds, too.

– watches the occasional movie that doesn't have the words terminate, blow-up, expel or kill in the title.

– carries tissue in his pocket.

– is able to tie his own tie.

– can sense when it's time to leave a party.

– takes his baseball cap off for the national anthem and classy restaurants.

– does not use his car as a portable trash can.

– doesn't receive subscription magazines that come in plain, unmarked, brown envelopes.

– is competitive
and compassionate.

– notices new outfits, glasses and hair color.

– does not save his entire reading repertoire for the bathroom.

– takes turns getting up at night when the baby cries.

– does not lick his fingers while eating supper.

– knows, but never tells, your bra
and shoe size.

– doesn't think that a play is only something that happens in football.

– stays calm even when he discovers a new dent in his car.

– doesn't consider dinner preparations as looking through the yellow pages.

– Knows that the word "committed" doesn't always mean straight jackets and rubber rooms.

– is not embarrassed to buy feminine hygiene products.

– doesn't think love is just a way to keep score in tennis.

– knows that a goose is a barnyard animal, not something to be given to you when you are in front of him in the check out line.

– seldom displays his dinner menu on his tie or facial hair.

– knows at least three clean jokes.

– writes thank you cards.

– always opens the car door,
but makes sure his barn
door is shut before he
leaves the house.

– realizes that beds are for sleeping, reading and making love, but not suitable for crackers, chips or microwave popcorn.

– empties the dishwasher.

– can read, spell and pronounce words that have more than four letters in them.

– never decorates a driveway with the contents of an ashtray.

– does not try to impress the in-laws by burping the alphabet.

– not only can huddle, but can snuggle and cuddle too.

– does not wear spandex.

– does not entertain the family at supper time by opening his full mouth and saying, "Train wreck—recognize anyone?"

– never ever picks his nose, butt, teeth or any other anatomical structure in public.

– takes the dog to the vet.

– does not blow his nose like a foghorn.

– chews with his mouth closed.

– has attended an aerobics class and has watched the ballet, but has never worn tights.

– Helps put up and take down the Christmas tree.

– is not proud of gastric distress.

– cries once in a while.

– does not do his financial planning at the race track.

129

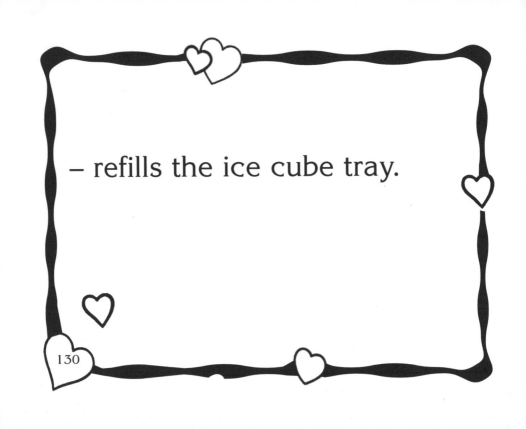

– refills the ice cube tray.

– knows that a yellow light means "slow down", not "step on the gas."

131

– irons his own shirts.

– brakes for school buses and squirrels.

– slides the seat forward
after driving your car.

– looks before uttering the words, "Where are my...."

– empties his pants pockets before throwing them into the wash.

– doesn't jingle the change in his pocket.

– isn't so cheap that he only calls 1-800 numbers, and isn't so desperate that he only calls 1-900 ones.

– does not believe that blue angels are heavenly.

– never talks on a cell phone while driving.

– does not feel that interior decorating constitutes proudly displaying the newest plastic promotional-toy from a fast food restaurant.

– can be interrupted even
during a sports cast.

– helps his kids with
their homework.

143

– can make beds, paper bag lunches and good money.

– knows where the greeting card store is.

145

– doesn't lose keys, wallets, kids' birthdays or your respect.

– knows that being faithful
means more than being full
of faith that he won't
get caught.

147

– never goes into your purse or diary.

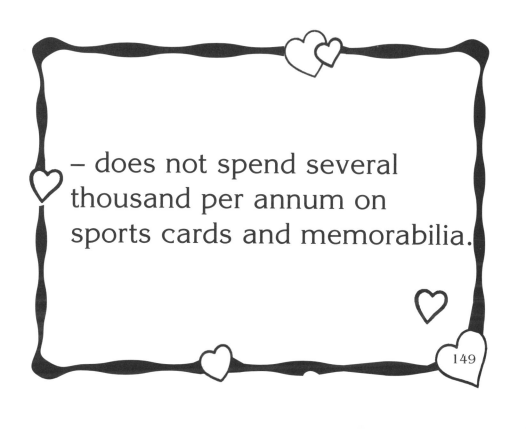

– does not spend several thousand per annum on sports cards and memorabilia.

149

– stays in shape.

– graduated from something.

151

– always changes the toilet paper roll immediately after he empties it.

– stomps out ring around the collar and ring around the tub, but not ring around your finger.

– doesn't chew his nails, grind his teeth or drool.

– can say "I love you" without choking or going into cardiac arrest.

– doesn't do his Christmas shopping at garage sales.

156

– is wanted, but not by a collection agency.

– does not believe that underwear and socks are a household uniform.

158

– doesn't call you "Honey"
only when he
wants something.

– is able to sleep in on the weekend, or, if not, is able to let you sleep in on the weekend.

– knows the difference between clothing and tatoos.

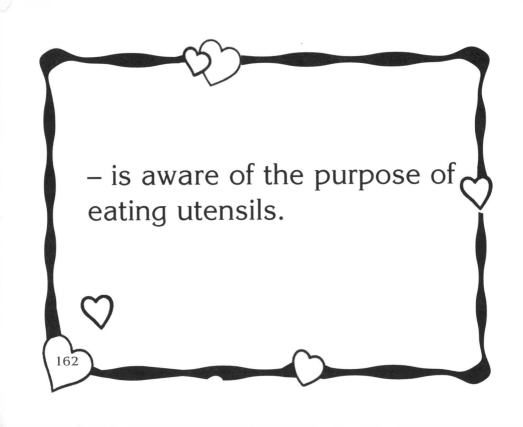

– is aware of the purpose of eating utensils.

– employs air freshener after having to use the words "pollute", "toxic" or is speechless when describing a restroom experience.

– doesn't lie to look good.

– goes to the dentist at least once a year.

– knows at least one poem other than a limerick.

– sends roses.

Other Titles by Great Quotations

201 Best Things Ever Said
The ABC's of Parenting
African-American Wisdom
As A Cat Thinketh
The Best of Friends
The Birthday Astrologer
Chicken Soup
The Cornerstones of Success
Daddy & Me
Fantastic Father, Dependable Dad
For Mother, A Bouquet of Sentiments
Global Wisdom
Golden Years, Golden Words
Grandma, I Love You
Growing Up in Toyland
Happiness Is Found Along the Way
Hollywords
Hooked on Golf
In Celebration of Women
Inspirations
Interior Design for Idiots
I'm Not Over the Hill
The Lemonade Handbook
Let's Talk Decorating
Life's Lessons
Life's Simple Pleasures
A Lifetime of Love
A Light Heart Lives Long

Midwest Wisdom
Mommy & Me
Mrs. Aesop's Fables
Mother, I Love You
Motivating Quotes for Motivated People
Mrs. Murphy's Laws
Mrs. Webster's Dictionary
My Daughter, My Special Friend
The Other Species
Parenting 101
The Perfect Man
Reflections
Romantic Rhapsody
The Rose Mystique
The Secret Language of Men
The Secret Language of Women
The Secrets in Your Name
Social Disgraces
Some Things Never Change
The Sports Page
Sports Widow
Stress or Sanity
A Teacher Is Better Than Two Books
TeenAge of Insanity
Thanks from the Heart
Things You'll Learn...
Wedding Wonders
Working Woman's World

GREAT QUOTATIONS PUBLISHING COMPANY

Glendale Heights, IL 60139
Phone (630) 582-2800 • Fax (630) 582-2813